November St. Michael

Lover's Rhetoric

The Ramblings Of A Woeful Heart

A POETRY COLLECTION

He—Brews Publishing, LLC.

November St. Michael
Lover's Rhetoric:
The Ramblings Of A Woeful Heart

ISPN: 978-1-71600-428-5

Manufactured in the United States of America

Ms. T. Simmons
1975-2008

Preface

This collection of poetry was written in honor of my first idea of love. It was personified in a woman I grew very fond of. The conversations and intimacy we shared will stay with me for as long as I shall live and love. This is a work that displays raw emotion before, during, and after pertinent events occurred in our lives.

It is within these pages that I describe and exhaustively express how trying to maintain a relationship and remain optimistic towards the future, whatever that may have been. My emotions here, are verbalized by way of the heart. This volume of poetry precedes quite a bit of my previously published collections. This was at a more innocent time. One in which, I had no experience or knowledge of an outcome for the things one could expect, when they did not come to fruition. And then reality takes center stage and totally commands your attention and, totally dismisses any ideals of how love is supposed to play out.

If ever there was a theme to my work, this one blared "change." I say that as I was forever changed by it all. And though I would experience heartbreak in later years, it was this relationship that prepared me for it. Although, the pain is always excruciating and there is always a lesson to be learned. The most important thing is to gather yourself completely, and collect the pieces with the remembrance that this is why you are supposed to take love seriously. It was the rhetoric from this love and its failure that made things become so—rhetorical in the first place. Then again--what do I really know?

Contents

Chapter 1- Fantastic Sorrow

Request Granted....13
Prelude To A Breakup....14
Cold Turkey....16
I Love You....18
Horror Scope....19
That Scent....21
Too Much....22
A Breakup....24
Gullible Lullaby....26
The Pain Of Love....28
Love Sick....31
Your Pillow Is Waiting....33
Love Lost....34
Lesley....35

Chapter 2 - Happily Angry

The Contents Of A New Day....39
Listening....40
Fruits And Vegetables....41
Chest Examination....42
Ground....43

Chest Examination (Part 2)....................44
Declaration Of A Worker Bee..............48
Men, Women, and Heaven...............50
Ciao Mi Amour (Goodbye My Love).........51

Chapter 3 — Comedic Tragedy

Another New Day.............................55
Pleasantries......................................56
Alright...57
Chest Examination (Part 3)......................58
Being Uncomfortable With Happiness.......59
Nothing Else To Say........................60
Map..61
Experiences Of Love.......................62
An Imaginary Argument........................64
Single Value................................66
vs..67
I Miss My Ex...68
Her...69
Hushed..74
The whY...75
Some Nerve................................76
Your Funeral.............................77

November St. Michael

Lover's Rhetoric

The Ramblings Of A Woeful Heart

A POETRY COLLECTION

1

Fantastic Sorrow

request granted

She asked the poet to write her a poem
yet, while he loved her nothing materialized

When she wandered away, the words introduced
themselves now, she has several to choose from

However; by this point she wasn't around to read them
someone else distracted her from the art

prelude to a breakup

My first love was fictitious
but my "first" will always by my "first"
but now I'm ready for "seconds"
at least the ones that add up to the minute
when I realized you were not the one for me
and likewise
our time has passed
what could have been—would have been
had we been more mature

Love is clear
but, I'm not
and you think yours—is
but, true hearts don't lie
men do
Only the foolish rush into things
with their eyes closed
behind
blind folds

I am a man
no different from any other man
I've just been in denial
about denying it

I love you
I do
I love you and
I—I—think I love a few others
I'm not being ungrateful
just weary
weary about being unfaithful
due to the things my fate shows
and I know your intuition as of late told—
you that something is different
some things are different
I'm changing
you've already changed
and you're chained
to remain here
near your ancestor's remains
I am not linked to anything here
maybe… anyone (if that makes sense)

I'll wait a period of time
to see if you get your period on time
if so
I go
if not I'm locked
but, it would only be temporary for me
and I'd hate to add to your
already "double life sentence"
I don't want to be the cause
of your inability to succeed
so let us utilize wisdom
Our separation would only fortify
the friendship that never was
fore we were lovers
before we were anything other
but then again… I'm speaking out of anger

cold turkey

Momentary attacks
plague my system
I feel I need her
I need to feel her
and fill her with me
until I am full

This addiction to her is debilitating
the yearning is unparalleled
Suffer me
Dear Lord
I am suffering
nothing seems to comfort me

Comforting
thoughts in my mind
minding
about her mind
and whether it is on me

This love makes me cringe
only her presence
can satisfy this binge
but the relationship is long distance
when she's away
and when she's close
she is still some distance away

What's going on
with these on goings
that I'm not aware of
they worry me
Worrying
about her pauses
stopping without warning
I brace myself
but find nothing
or rather no one to hold on to
Facing a head on collision
with reality

Love is the worst drug to be addicted to
it—claims the lives of people each day
and I'm addicted too
dependency not withstanding
I want to stand with her
but she doesn't play fair

She had the advantage
supplying me with herself
one sample at a time
getting me hooked on the idea of us
however; her silence means she wants to cease
I can't stop
not until I'm at peace
or deceased
There are no meetings
for lovers anonymous
I am—
on my own

i love you

I love you
my eyes love you
my nose loves you
my ears love you
my mouth loves you
my hands love you
I love you

I love you on the inside
so much that it shows on the outside
how much that I love you
inside and out
I love you with or without you
I can't stop loving you
wouldn't stop
couldn't stop
shouldn't stop loving you
believe me I have tried

I have cried "I love you"
more than a thousand times
and for the thousandth time
I love you

The only thing
that could ever come
between you and I
is—love

horror scope

… never really believed in astrology
For what?
They're nothing more than rash generalizations
about a person's characteristics
based on when they were born
It's all rubbish

Boys will be boys until manhood creeps up
girls will be women every chance they get
so by the time maturity kicks in they're pretty much
accustomed to it

All humans have a common bond
I once bonded with a young lady
whom was uncommonly human
flawed and fallible
(She's a Capricorn)
I knew nothing of bonds which is not common
It's almost inhuman
Naïve and contradictory
(I'm a Scorpio)
She drove my sex drive

I like her
I love her too
I love liking her

She loves me
She likes me too
She likes loving me

but she is not like me
we are unlikely
even though we like each other
and we love each others—likes

define this love of ours
and things get difficult
yet the signs are there

We can hold one another
like a deep breath
Death and stress has brought her to the surface

meanwhile I act as if
I don’t need air
her share has been much greater than my half
though there are times when
she can’t handle a whole portion
of my giving when it’s given

during the day we are slaves to the Sun
but at night she is the dark sky
with a smile that resembles the constellations

I lay under her
willingly—ready to read into things

that scent

Laying there next to her
one night in particular
Nothing special
He was watching TV
and glimpsed at her
Admiring her beauty
but what he didn't know
was that she was doing the same
relinquishing her attraction
towards him without saying a word
Her body chemistry had been mixing
glands were activated
dilating pores
interrupting fresh air
with the concentration of that scent

He smelled the anticipation of her passion
her human fragrance
it was as loud as potpourri
naturally ushering his arousal
reveling in the aroma he smiles sheepishly
and tells her of his discovery
outing her lustful sensibility
she blushes--embarrassed by his exactness
they have a flirtatious exchange

All is innocent yet, she darts to the living room
to be alone
so her body can calm down

too much

The young lady was accustomed to tough love
until the day a man came along
casually not trying to rush love
however, he was love sick
and she loved it
but what does love have to do with—
a hug
a kiss
and the bashful smiles that coincide
with a blush
something a rush of blood gives
proceeding loves' gifts

Animal attraction
like a pup's love
Tails wagging in the morning to wake up love
heavy panting in the evening to break up love
to the young lady this was rough love
the stuff of—dreams
beautiful scenes she hadn't seen too much of
yet, the man was keen on feelings
a touch
could lead them to clutch love
By now the young lady was close to him
but had no such love
before
she had tough love
before
she did not trust love

no such luck just love
until this love
his love
she thought this was too much love
while he assumed it was just enough love

The young lady was accustomed to tough love
abrupt love
the kind that would always interrupt love
Yes, she was young but she needs to understand grown
up love

a breakup

Four days before Christmas
it happened
so—expectedly
over the phone for reasons unknown
or just beyond petty
I was jilted…passed over
you moved on
in need of a husband

A husband to take care of you and yours
so you don't have to work
for several months at a time
what a waste of time
wasting much of your mind

Big penises and multiple orgasms
don't equate to a soul mate
neither does a good job with benefits
Tell me…would a two story house with two cars
in a two car garage
and a dog jumping and wagging
really make you happy
because you weren't happy… right?
That's what you said when you called
(fill in profanity here____!!!)
but immaturity aside I'll settle down

Your indiscretions led to mine
all I ever wanted to do was

make you mine
you spoiled things (as usual)
ruined things with your mentality
you're never wrong
but your decisions have always proved otherwise
I did right by you
and would even write about you
Tell you ever little and large thing
I liked about you

Now I really see how much
I was right about you
praying out loud at night
to Christ about you
in spite of you despitefully using me
after one year and six months
of being official
the issues, and "haircuts" deemed sacrificial,
the I love yous and I love you toos,
hugs, kisses, saliva, sweat, blood, tears,
semen, and one of your earrings

it ends—just like that?

With us not being friends
not being enemies
not being anything
but a memory

gullible lullaby

She was a naïve girl
Tell her what she wants to hear
and she'll give you what you want to feel
Her father was blind
so he couldn't see what she was becoming
Her mother had a habit
and didn't even notice what she was doing
her older brother bloomed late
while her older sister developed the some habitual
demons her mother had, but for another thing

This naïve girl
had no good examples
so she picked up a habit of her own
She figured sex was the answer
so sleeping in any bed made her
feel closer to home
Indulging herself with men and more men
she even took a boy and turned him into a man
before long--she had her own little boy
and would have had another little one
but stillbirths feel worse
than the ones people volunteer to kill first
but time heals all wounds
and her small womb
consumed more volume
and pretty soon confusion ensues
a little girl was to be born possibly to two fathers
both unaware to the others existence

Naïve girl
a mother contingent
on the outcome and out came a daughter
Who is the father
why bother
She goes on going on

Naïve girl
A damsel named Delilah
eyeing Eve's world
like a delightful Jezebel
The consummate whore
partaking in extramarital affairs
Why stone her
when one can take her home
and know her
This—naïve girl

I hope her daughter
doesn't follow the path
bestowed to her
by the Grandmother, Aunt, and Mother
and all the other
unscrupulous souls
her dear mother has her hover
around
falling asleep to the subtle sounds
of a gullible lullaby

the pain of love

To M'lady love—
if you're listening
you were my crucifixion
labor pangs
A major pain
my favorite pain
Eight long years I suffered
I loved you and hated you too
but I hated hating you

This heart has your face on it
These lungs long for your breath
as each eye searches
for a glimpse of your tortured beauty
You teased me
when you fooled yourself
into thinking you'd need me
Believe me
because I believed you
Believed in you
Me and you
You and I
Us
Together
Forever

Never
You had better plans
with a better man

whom could take better care
of you better than this veteran
Well-seasoned is your ways
of how you work and play
and your sway (physically and spiritually)
It's always been like you
to have your way
like a wayward stray
I become your prey maybe because I didn't pray

But there's no turning back
to your turning back
Lazily tattooed and emblazoned with those
"luscious lips"
I used to touch and kiss
I—I was making love
while you were just having sex
I would have never imagined
anything such as this
could hurt so bad

I—I was investing time
while you were biding yours
You used me
lied openly
and was obvious about it
I was oblivious to it
I have a right to be disappointed
You owe me more than an apology
ante up
I'll see you again
and when you see me again
begin to notice the improvements within

a man renewed in his skin
and then you'll realize while
you're standing beside the better man
that—he isn't me
and I am the man
that would have been much more…

lovesick

I'm tired of love

I don't think I can love again
because my heart seems empty
Broken so much it just won't heal right
Full of holes
everything I put in
Leaks out

I'm tired of love

I know it's a cold world
but I'm freezing
My will to live
is my will to love
so why does love keep leaving me

Love doesn't love me
even though I love… love
God is love— right?
so maybe it's just me

I'm sorry Lord
I can't feel you through all this
like I should
I'm in so much pain
it hurts
This hurts
I think I'm lovesick

hunger pains
muddled thoughts of suicide
are interrupted by good sense
and the hope I need
to get me through this break up

your pillow is waiting

Desperate arms search for you
but emptiness is their reward
alarming the sense of touch
the darkness in the room
is relieved by moonlight
illuminating
the shadows that become
night mirages of you
laying here
on your side of the bed
embracing your pillow
dormant
inhaling… exhaling
to watch you sleep is exhilarating
vast amounts of kisses were stolen
while you were dreaming
dreaming… dream—

your image is flickering
during these wee hours
in this room
now containing one
submitting to tears
and petitioning for sleep
along side a vacant pillow

love lost

The trust is gone
The attraction has waned
fading before two beating hearts
that once shared melodies
everything that was, has diminished
except—the love
which is not gone
just misplaced

Lesley

Being physical
with you finally
after Larry
during Tonya
wasn't the mistake
giving ourselves to them
instead of each other was—
had we obeyed our course
of nature early on
Neither of them
would have existed

Now—
You are with this other guy
and she is engaged to marry
some stranger
I am however
left to ponder the meaning
of being alone
The two of you exemplify
the difference
between irony and coincidence
Although, you my dear Lesley
were the prelude to all of my fantastic sorrow

2

Happily Angry

the contents of a new day

Awaking
before the early bird yawns
the Sun is still groggy
I bid the Lord good morning
by voicing an appreciation
for the blessing of living another tomorrow
and making one more request
for forgiveness
due to slumbering trespasses

Amens
are followed by hygiene performances
whispered readings of loud scriptures
and daily nourishment
with the new day's foundation set
one can now be constructive
by earning a value for self
and the privilege to frolic
whenever time deems it permissible
During the course of this new day
I take a moment to remember
I must be focused

listening

It boggles my mind
how much more
I'm listening to you now
than when we were together
Often times reflection can be blaring
My Mother always told me that
when it comes to women
a man should be a good listener
to win her
Well—I'm listening
and… have been for quite some time
but ever since you left
I listen much better
to your voice as it constantly echoes
across canyons of thought

Your absence even makes
dead silence resonate
Here I am tuning in for anything
The phone
The door
or even the mailman

It boggles my mind
how much more
I'm listening to you now
especially, when reminiscing
tends to reveal one's mistakes
Provoking the realization that it is too—late

fruits and vegetables

Gotta' take the good with the bad
because believe it or not
they're both good for us
providing the vital nutrients
that love needs to grow
and go further or—farther
I don't know which one
maybe both

Whatever it takes to stay close
relationships these days
don't seem to be meant to last
built too fast
so they crumble even quicker
bad times are gonna' come
they can either get better or bitter

Something people should consider
when they first meet
of course, at first it's sweet
and we all want more
but elapse the hours
and try to swallow what's sour
and that will be the evidence
determining if your love is pure

chest examination

I am complicated
difficult to get along with
I am sorry and I apologize
to all who've been affected by my attitude
plagued with the saddest mood
more often than pleasant
excuse my irreverence
karma usually comes around with severance
and the events in my life are the symptoms of this
Love exits
to let others enter

These are the trials that come into play
during the troubled Winter
of another sinner
one that looks desperately to the future of sainthood
in Springtime
before the Summer simmers
insomnia and loss of appetite
gives the false appearance of a younger... slimmer
version of myself but illusions evaporate
quicker than the gasp it takes
to take in who I really am
this is my stethoscope

ground

During our season together
I've sown seeds in other gardens
while we were planting our own
watered them frequently
or at times when I felt others desire this seed
Happening when you hid
behind clouds
and I lacked your sunlight
so—
artificial alternatives were provided
whether I wanted them or not
however, none of these incandescent luminaries
could ever outshine your rays
All in all
I did my share of dirt
cautious not to disturb our Earth
your ground was never hurt
because I knew its worth
but you were moonlighting
and we're soon fighting
over property
improperly
I lose
and you choose
to go with what another proprietor is offering
pondering as I'm wandering
about—
on empty land

chest examination (part II)

What is it about me that no one likes
my hygiene is fine
so could it be the stench of my attitude
maybe
possibly
probably
however, I always thought of myself as a nice guy
reserved and shy with a wavering confidence
embarrassed by compliments
devastated by insults
is it low self-esteem
maybe
possibly
probably
however, I feel like I have no self-esteem
I try to love everybody
and I do mean try
and I do mean everybody
I give my love freely
Am I simple
Am I really the naïve one
maybe
possibly
probably
however, people have been known to ask me for advice
Did I say that I was nice
well…?
I meant too nice

I get that from my mother
when I decide to be stern about something
others take it out of context
Is it my sarcastic retorts
maybe
possibly
probably
however, sarcasm has become
my best defense mechanism
due to years of solitude
and social abuse by way of ridicule
and the association with inconsistent peers
Do my words hurt
maybe
possibly
probably
however, I usually speak out
after being injured emotionally
I'm not justifying it
I'm just defining it
out of all of God's children am I the worst?
maybe
possibly
probably
however, how could I ever doubt his mercy
I guess because I know I'm unworthy
by being too worldly
a late bloomer
whom has never experienced anything too early
yet, the things I did partake of were always in excess
overweight and undereducated
misunderstood and underestimated
The pitiful thing about me borders on desperation
no stethoscope
ever invented can tell a man the contents of his heart

My evils have humbled me
crumbled me
into fetal positions mumbling
irreconcilable contradictions among myself
Have I been dreaming too long?
maybe
possibly
probably
however, dreams have been known to come true
that is if enough ambition comes through
when one comes to
otherwise it's deferred
(Langston's word)
or it is all together shattered
Time escapes me if I concentrate too hard
because deep thought crosses
that continuum in momentary intervals
which can spawn ideas, inspiration, and epiphanies
the music in symphonies and brand new inventions
for the betterment of mankind or the exact opposite
I often think
staring at my exact opposite
watching him mock me
perfectly—regarding the memory of a lover
that's still hurting me
That wound is still fresh
still wet
from the heartbreak of a heart
that has since been stilled—
yes
it feels just like near death
Will things get better for me?
maybe
possibly
probably

however, I must rise
wipe my eyes
and survive because I'm alive
A life that lives remembers to give
and give graciously
I keep telling myself to pray for me
as well as others
my mother
her mother
other mothers
their sons and daughters
and the fathers
those present or unaccounted for
I can't lie to myself anymore
especially if I'm going to consider myself honest
"purge me O' Lord"
as I'm examining my—self

declaration of a worker bee

What do I do now
now, that I'm single and single-mindedly
drowning myself in work

More work
Mr. Smart's youngest son told me
that I should become a worker so, I work

More work
God's work
Hard work
Yard work
Large work

I work until the job's done and my goals are met
Employed at two places
I'm off to work

Working it out
while, I work through pain
in pain

More work
Hard work
School work
Home work
House work

After work, I work out
to help my muscles get stronger
I'm looking better as I get healthier

All of this is done
so I can work longer
Meet the new me

Men love to work
I will be your best example
working more now so, I can work less later

Years after the labor
being careful not to work myself to death
throughout stress

awarding myself with the harvest
yet, the real reward is when others
appreciate the work

More work
Hard work
No more—
I work SMARTER

Thank you sir

me, women, and Heaven

The only thing that stands between
Heaven
me and is women

The flesh is a weak thing
physically I look strong
but indeed, I'm a weakling
temptations like drugs or alcohol
never hopped on my back
none of those just—women
black women
other women
that "woman"

I'm scared because this road leads to where
I'm not trying to go
Oh! This is my woe
thus, are the ways of a young man
wanting to please God
yet, is enslaved in the lust
that displays no more hope

I'm emptying my heart
Dear Reader—so excuse me as I pour slow
Lord knows
women are what I adore so
Therefore, I search for a sanctified one
to court and marry
that is until—the whores show

ciao mi amour (Goodbye My Love)

If you really love me
you would have loved me

Your actions said otherwise
and I hate you for that

However, I do love you for this—
and that's for… ever loving me at all

I suppose this is truly farewell
so I must love you goodbye

3
Comedic Tragedy

another new day

Before the eyes can exercise their use
the conjecture of this day is set

The Good Lord's graciousness is entertained
earnestly, however; rising does not happen immediately

only the indefatigable
thought of expectation

"...careless yesterdays leave a residue"
I think

Yet, this is another day's genesis
nothing right now is permanent

because no motions have been made
history at this point is a blank page

so before its author moves to write
let him be—mindful

pleasantries

Verbally pleasing
pleasure seekers
see through
the smiles
that beam
wide… clean
lines that
happiness brings
tides of
good things

alright

Unsure and insecure
I shouldn't be but, I am
because you've exhausted my trust
you say "stop assuming"
but, how can I while this love is still consuming
every part of me

Let me show you how much I will sacrifice
and love you whole heartedly
forgive me for whatever
whenever you can pardon me
this can't be over
I want to finish what we started—please

Second chances
make for better romances
The kisses are sweeter
and embraces last longer
making us stronger
I need you back in my life

at the front
as my wife
side by side
us together
Is that alright?

chest examination (part III)

After pondering the maybes
analyzing the possibilities
and scrutinizing what was truly probable

I stand in front of the mirror (again)
seeing things clearer
reflecting on this reflection
of imperfection
searching my heart for the part
infected with affections
confessions
lead me to make some adjustments
questioned myself
and well… self answered with some suggestions
adjusting my discussion
to a one word subject… change

Yes
I can change
I will change
I must change
I want to change
and I will keep changing

until the day comes when I know that
I've been changed
That way a more valiant man
can take charge
and show a difference

being uncomfortable with happiness

Happiness is a luxury
It comes—It goes
it is the pretense to true, insurmountable joy
many are pillaged of

To be happy is most uncomfortable
because one never knows when
it is going to cease and usher in
another bout of misery

oft' times happiness
isn't recognized until it ventures away
leaving only the anticipation
of its always brief return

nothing else to say

Words are eternal
like a—a spiritual music
all things seem to speak to one another
one way or another

Communication can be the most simplest of sounds
just listen to the inhabitants of Earth
talk to us and each other

Tune in to the universe
and experience the conversations
between
heavenly bodies

Therefore, realizing when a couple
that was once paired together
only to split from their shared unit,
should be incapable of silence

The heart can be broken
and bleeding and even stop beating
but not loving

Emotions use motion
to describe themselves
so there should never come a time
when two people who've loved each other

have nothing else to say

Map

… no guide on this tour
to tell me
that between her legs
is the wrong direction
to her heart

There's freedom in the North

Thoughts… matter

and a penis
is a poor substitute

for a compass

experiences of love

Before I ever knew love
I had love
grew up to love—through love

My first love I thought was true love
but, went unrequited like unapproved love
filled with brief kisses and a few hugs

Now, I yearn for the romance of a new love
but, it hides and is hard to find
I remember a friend of mine

and how he would constantly misconstrue love
with quite a few lovers
women of every color

which, is how he confused love
we would ride together… going where ever
On the night he told me all this we cried together

exiting the car, changed this mind of mine forever
not wanting to experience that, when I find my treasure

I remember a young lady
once told me that she didn't "have time for love"
unwilling to see the signs of love

She wasn't inclined to love
as I'd opine about that intoxicating wine of love

the kind of love
that's unconditional and not traditional
unlike my last love that was fictional

after that I hated love
because it would not love me
even though I love being within it

Love hurts when it leaves
painfully reoccurring when I see couples
I stare at love

self pity leads me to ask "where is love"
So when it's my turn to tell someone about this
I will say that I am scared of love

This way
they will remember it
when their season is due

an imaginary argument

You never loved me
you said—you did
but deep down you didn't
listen
who are we kiddin'
I've tried and tried
to reach those places
inside your heart
that you've kept hidden

If it's over for good then—good
Goodbye
good riddance
it's not fair to me that I keep trying
while you keep lying
to me, as well as yourself
about this thing called us

{Lower your voice}

Why fuss
we're adults and should
be able to discuss
why our plus
is now a minus
You tell me to put the past behind us

Why?
when you continue
to do the same things
you did back then as if you're trying to rewind us
multiplying those problems
that eventually divided us

I'm wishin'
you'd listen
because you always seem
to lose the point in transition
by reading two things
into every one statement I make
which makes things worse
Try thinking twice, first--
lest you continue
to take what is said out of context

single value

I am single
very single
like—a one dollar bill
motivating my willingness to change

that way I'll have
something quarterly
to keep me company
when loneliness doesn't make much sense

vs.

Is it—
me vs. her or you vs. him
when my verse is slim
her song is long
about my wrongs
completely stifling
her being trifling
so I extended my notes and wrote out
my love in quotes to quell
the splintering of what got broke

Is it—
him vs. her or you vs. me
when she curses me
I raise my voice
now unsure of the day I made this choice
but eventually we must agree
while there is still enough of us to see
I say it's up to her
and she says that it's up to me

Is it—
she vs. him or he vs. she
both of us need to free the breeze
before the air we share
is no longer ours but, theirs…
the new pair of people
we'll choose to get over each other
which in the end won't seem fair

i miss my ex

Every day I see a face
I haven't seen in a while
separated by more than a few miles
a new marriage and a new child
my feelings have not dwindled
but are instead gathered in a shrewd pile

I miss my ex

her face
her eyes
and that cute smile
that beguiled
my masculine wiles

her

This black woman
had a smooth, dark skin tone
it was like God glazed her entire body
with a shimmering dark enamel

Her smile embodied the sweet humility
of everything innocent and pure
that's when I met her
when I was not yet "experienced"

A 21 year old male, still a virgin
in the later part of the 21rst century
was considered somewhat of a rarity
an odyssey

a mythical creature by today's standards
I was sort of a saint when I met her—the sinner
well on my way to becoming a sinner

sexually a novice
willful beginner
attracted to her especially, her body
it was built sturdy like a mare

I was "The Rocking Horse Winner"
that girl
this—dark skinned black girl
had my nose open
whenever I'd close my eyes

I was revealed things
I'd only seen a few times
as a result of scenes
I saw once in my youth
my love was just as immediate
as the climaxes she commandeered

unfortunately these meetings
of temporary euphoria led the way to common fears
uncommon tears
problem years

seasonal flings
that would sting
now or later
here or there

on and off
life's unfair
because like that mare
she would kick back notions of togetherness

a heartbreak aches
leaving me in a state
of love and hate

before she returned
I learned to yearn
but that too burns
when there is no return

Time—
goes by
goodbye
by gone time

brief intermissions
transform into
long winter mingling
I continue to do single things

Signaling
to other single females
but it didn't do one single thing
but single her out

another attempt at love
lingered her doubts
but the word's out
she is with child (again)

not by me
but by him
I sighed and cried
an unrhymed hymn

because love sure can blind men
and bind limbs
by why HIM
why not—me

I'm a good man
yet, as a man I went on
to do no good
and went wild

because of him having her
and her having his child
I'm almost misogynistic now
massaging misfits now

promiscuous me
I did this—Wow!
lowered my standards
accepting anything

with or without proper manners
or grammar
nothing mattered
I miss sinning with my original mistress

but the distress of just sex
made me miss being a saint
I guess sex just impressed me
with the freshly

wet pictures it would paint
only later to taint
my impression of a woman and her being genuine
I felt like I could not trust her

therefore, I could not trust them
struggling for redemption
I would tempt her
with another attempt at us

to make her a permanent fixture
in my life but by the tenth word
it didn't work
a married man came along

and sang a song of sweet nothings (to her)
I feel something sick swell up in the nothingness
where my heart once was accustomed to a comfy fit

but no longer
now it's quick to love
pumping it
throughout my body

and hers
and others
among others
I shudder

at the fact of how I clutter
together lovers
that have no idea I harbor
what lovers lack

and that
is the lack to love
I couldn't… tried
but didn't

wanted to
but went on being unwanted
well—a few did
I just didn't need what they wanted

after I got what I wanted
another year, another attempt
I have contempt for her
because I keep trying

hushed

Trying to find the words
when you have so many to choose from
becomes fruitfully arduous

yet, well-chosen words are useless
when ears don't exist
so silence just seems easier

the why

whY is a question
that often cannot be answered
or just—isn't
even when it can be
so I leave it alone
allowing it to lie there
between a mystery and sleep

some nerve

Privately I chuckled to myself
when I heard the news
that you had passed

Privately I snickered amongst myself
upon hearing the news
I remember you called me twice
and I let the phone ring
wrestling myself not to answer
thinking silence would best express
what I didn't have to say to you

Privately I wept to myself
after the shock set in
realizing the truth to that news
I want to talk to you now
but, I am devoid of your voice
I shutter and shake my head
because of all the stunts to pull and
without even as much as uttering it—
"Death" was your last word
unspoken to me
dying suddenly is so you I think tearfully

"You got some nerve."

your funeral

The day of your funeral
I sat five rows away from your casket
wearing my black pen striped suit
my mother bought me about a year or so ago

My hair grew back to the long flowing loc's
that you loved combing your fingers through
to re-up your attraction to me but, this-
happened

Quentin came with me to see you
"Pooky" performed a praise dance
Tracey acted as you would imagine she'd act

Khaleed looked optimistic
but, your daughter appeared to be lost
your friends were distant

I saw your mom and she looked numb
having lost your father four years earlier
now… you
your sister is a wreck
and your brother is hiding his pain as usual

I listened to your husband
try his best to eulogize you
however, he was long winded and lacked
the poetic sentiment I would've provided

seeing as how I used
to wrap you up with my words
as you lay there just far enough for me to see
you as sleeping not--dead

I met you in this very church eleven years ago
and we saw each other in this church last
and now, I will see you last in this church

I will not go to your gravesite
'fore upon a time once,
we would make love in long, hot showers

and it because of that…

I refuse
to watch
anyone
throw dirt on you

other works

Rhetorical Lover (2014)

Rhetorical Lover (2016)
{Revisited}

Rhetorical Lover (TBA)
Soul Ties With Stale Mates

November St. Michael

Social Media

Twitter:
@ til_November
Instagram:
@november_stmichael

He—Brews Publishing, LLC.

P.O. Box 3446
Hampton, VA. 23663

Thank you for your support.

www.ingramcontent.com/pod-product-compliance
Lightning Source LLC
Chambersburg PA
CBHW021340060726
47591CB00006B/2117

* 9 7 8 1 7 1 6 0 0 4 2 8 5 *